C000135772

SOVIET INTELLIGENCE COMMUNICATIONS [1952]

FEDERAL BUREAU OF INVESTIGATION

NIMBLE BOOKS LLC: THE AI LAB FOR BOOK-LOVERS

~ FRED ZIMMERMAN, EDITOR ~

Humans and AI making books richer, more diverse, and more surprising.

Publishing Information

(c) 2024 Nimble Books LLC

ISBN: 978-1-60888-230-4

AI-generated Keyword Phrases

- Soviet intelligence communication methods
- Open and clandestine communication channels in Soviet intelligence
- Soviet diplomatic couriers and intelligence transmission
- Secret sections in Soviet missions abroad
- Soviet intelligence cryptography and cipher systems
- Agent radio and clandestine communication networks
- Microdots and secret writing in Soviet espionage
- The Sorge network and Soviet intelligence communications
- Historical analysis of Soviet intelligence communication techniques
- Counterintelligence and Soviet communication channels

PUBLISHER'S NOTES

This is what the FBI knew in 1952 about how the Soviets communicated with their intelligence agents. Now you can fact-check OPPENHEIMER.

This annotated edition illustrates the capabilities of the AI Lab for Book-Lovers to add context and ease-of-use to manuscripts. In this publication, I experiment with a new package of AI abstracts that focus on helping the reader get (and share!) the gist: tldr (three words), tldr (vanilla); scientific style; as a catch phrase; and three different types of mnemonics: acronym, speakable, and singable. I might summarize these as "silly but pithy"! I continue to include tables of Notable Passages and Nutshell Summaries for each page in the document.

ANNOTATIONS

ABSTRACTS

TLDR (THREE WORDS)

Soviet spy communications.

TLDR (VANILLA)

Soviet intelligence used both open and clandestine communication channels. Open channels included enciphered cables and diplomatic couriers, while clandestine methods involved agent radio, couriers, and secret writing. The Sorge network in Japan relied heavily on radio communication and couriers to transmit information to Moscow.

SCIENTIFIC STYLE
Soviet Intelligence Communications: A Study of Open and Clandestine Methods

This study examines the communication methods employed by Soviet intelligence services, focusing on both open and clandestine channels. Open channels included enciphered cable and radio traffic transmitted through commercial facilities by Soviet diplomatic and trade establishments, as well as diplomatic couriers. Clandestine communication methods encompassed agent radio, couriers, and mail, including the use of microdots and secret writing.

The study details the procedures for handling secret communications at the Moscow headquarters of Soviet Military Intelligence (GRU), and describes the operation of "secret sections" within Soviet missions abroad, where communications were processed and secret files maintained. The use of cipher pads and code books for encrypting messages is also discussed.

The study highlights the case of the Sorge network in Japan, which relied heavily on clandestine radio operations and couriers to transmit intelligence to Moscow. Additionally, the network utilized 35mm film to convey documentary intelligence, a common practice in Soviet operations.

This study provides valuable insights into the complex and multifaceted communication methods employed by Soviet intelligence services, offering a deeper understanding of their operational techniques.

Keywords:

Soviet intelligence, communications, clandestine, open channels, diplomatic couriers, agent radio, microdots, secret writing, Sorge network, cryptography.

As a Catch Phrase

"From cables to couriers, the Soviets had a line on secrets."

Mnemonic

Soviet Intelligence Communications: Open and Clandestine
SICOOC

This mnemonic highlights the two main categories of communication channels used by **S**oviet **i**ntelligence: **O**pen (**c**ables, diplomatic **c**ouriers) and **C**landestine (agent radio, secret writing, microdots).

Remembering SICOOC can help you recall the key aspects of Soviet intelligence communication methods.

Mnemonic (Speakable)

Spies In Communication Often Operate Clandestinely

This mnemonic emphasizes the importance of clandestine communication methods in Soviet intelligence operations. It is designed to be easily spoken and remembered, similar to "My Dear Aunt Sally" for the order of operations in mathematics.

Mnemonic (Singable)

(Sing to the tune of "Twinkle, Twinkle Little Star")

> *Soviet spies, oh so sly,*
> *Communicate in ways so high,*
> *Open channels, cables fly,*
> *Secret sections, don't be shy.*
> *Clandestine ways, hidden deep,*
> *Agent radios, secrets keep,*
> *Microdots and secret ink,*
> *Information they will link.*
> *Soviet spies, oh so sly,*
> *Communicate in ways so high.*

This ditty highlights both open and clandestine communication methods used by Soviet intelligence, making it easier to remember the key points.

Page-by-Page Summaries

messages. Letters intercepted between New York, Buenos Aires, and Mexico City revealed Soviet intelligence efforts and the establishment of a radio link.

BODY-28   *CIA documents detail clandestine radio stations and Soviet networks in South America and Tokyo during WWII, highlighting the use of official channels and the need for studying communications in espionage operations.*

BODY-29   *Sorge, a journalist with a Communist history, operated as a spy in Tokyo with German cover, using couriers to pass film and funds to Moscow during WWII.*

BODY-30   *Sorge's spy network in Japan, including radio operator Max Klausen, was uncovered by Japanese police in 1941, revealing details of their operation and communication techniques.*

BODY-31   *Klausen, a Communist, built compact radio equipment in Japan for broadcasting, moving between different locations to avoid detection. His 100-watt equipment had a range of 1200 miles, with the control station believed to be in Eastern Siberia.*

BODY-32   *Klausen successfully evaded Japanese police detection by using various tactics, such as changing locations, transmission patterns, and equipment concealment.*

BODY-33   *Sorge and Klausen shared a cipher key in their Soviet operations, with Sorge teaching Klausen in 1938. They exchanged messages openly and added numbers to the basic cipher key for security.*

BODY-34   *Sorge network used German Statistical Yearbook for secure cipher, difficult to crack, Japanese authorities found house searches unproductive.*

BODY-35   *Sorge maintained radio contact with the Soviet station, transmitting thousands of words in 1939 and 1940. Despite liaison arrangements in 1940, he relied heavily on his agent radio. After the Russo-German War outbreak, Sorge reduced long reports and bulky documents.*

BODY-36   *Soviet intelligence networks in Western Europe during World War II heavily relied on secret agent radio communications, but many were eliminated or disrupted by German counterintelligence efforts, leading to breakdowns in communication and cooperation.*

BODY-37   *Soviet intelligence services were prepared for wartime conditions with portable wireless units, secret radio stations in Berlin, and intelligence activity against Germany directed from abroad.*

BODY-38   *Soviet spy networks in Western Europe relied on official channels until disrupted by German occupation, then used agent radio for contact with the "Centre."*

BODY-39   *German radio control organization rapidly silenced stations operated by the Trepper organization in Brussels in December 1941, leading to arrests, seizure of equipment, and integration of remaining members with another group. The new station operated until June 1942 when it was located and confiscated by the Germans.*

BODY-40   *German raid captures Communist Johann Wenzel, leading to deciphering of Soviet operations and exposure of network links, including Luftwaffe officer Schulze-Boysen's group with Soviet Trade Delegation agent. Technical difficulties hindered contact with "Centre" until agent dispatched from Brussels. Another group led by Arvid Harnack also uncovered.*

BODY-41   *Soviet intelligence groups in Europe failed to establish successful radio contact with the "Centre," leading to arrests and significant setbacks for Soviet intelligence operations.*

BODY-42   *Soviet spy Trepper compromised by German counterintelligence in 1942, escaped in 1943 but cooperated with Germans before fleeing. German counterintelligence tried* to use agent radios in France and Low Countries, with limited success. "Rote Drei" agent radio stations in Switzerland aided Soviet operation until late 1943.

BODY-43   German monitoring service intercepted secret information passing through Switzerland to Moscow during critical periods of World War II, leading to the identification and monitoring of the "Rote Drei" group, with the cipher not being broken until 1944. Alexander Rado played a key role in this espionage network.

BODY-44   Recruitment of Alexander Foote into Soviet intelligence during World War II, establishing radio communication network in Europe.

BODY-45   Foote established contact with Soviet control station in Switzerland, using fixed call signals and encrypted messages in five-digit groups, based on memorized key and statistical book codes, violating security rules by broadcasting for hours at a time.

BODY-46   Swiss authorities target "Rote Drei" network in 1943, find plain-text messages and enciphered versions. Foote's cipher compromised, but he continues to function. Swiss police raid Foote's transmitter, fail to playback station due to Rado's cipher. Control questions confirm suspicions of Soviet station.

BODY-47   Soviet intelligence operations in Switzerland and Sweden during WWII, including the 'Lucy' source and radio control section activities.

BODY-48   Soviet officials in Sweden operated radio stations to send military information to Moscow, with some stations already in contact with a control station near Moscow. One case involved a refugee named Lennart Katz who was caught transmitting data in 1942.

BODY-49   Technician Katz acted as a liaison for ciphered messages, using a cache in the countryside. The Soviets and Russians have used similar methods. In Sweden, radio technicians also performed cryptographic duties, with key books disguised as popular literature and dirty hands leaving smudges on code books.

BODY-50   Loss of valuable sources and networks due to reliance on agent radio in Western Europe during clandestine operations, with exception in Switzerland. Postwar, Soviet intelligence services improved training in agent radio technique, focusing on individual instruction and practice in Moscow.

BODY-51   Tips for camouflaging antennas in the theory and practice of radio direction finding, including disguising them as electrical wires or household items. Student agents instructed to limit transmissions to one hour. Concealment of equipment in furniture and secret compartments.

BODY-52   Soviet agent training included security methods, photography, cryptography, and compact agent radios like the "Tensor M" model. These radios were used in operations in Germany, Japan, Finland, and Western Europe, with units easily concealed in luggage.

BODY-53   Soviet agent-type radio equipment capable of transmitting long distances, easily concealed and transported, with weather-resistant burial capability for long-term use in satellite countries. Agent operators are trained and held in readiness with cipher systems and call schedules.

BODY-54   CIA operations in 1948 used agent radio and courier links to gather current information on Soviet methods, with agents bringing in radio equipment in secret and operating from private dwellings. Agents were provided with schedules for communication with the "Centre" in Moscow.

NOTABLE PASSAGES

BODY-4   *An ideal counterintelligence operation is the penetration of an adversary's communications between the service headquarters and the operating networks. It is this source which offers the most complete and most authentic account of the activities being conducted.*

BODY-6   *It might be noted, in this connection, that "secret sections" are established in all Soviet enterprises for the handling of secret papers and are said to function under regulations promulgated by the MGB. The secret section personnel, however, is recruited from the most trusted Party or Komsomol members in the particular enterprise and is not necessarily MGB personnel.*

BODY-7   *"Similarly, incoming messages were received in the code section, were deciphered, and distributed by the chief of the code section to the various chiefs of the operating sections."*

BODY-8   *These figures give a glimpse of the extent to which Soviet intelligence operations abroad rely upon enciphered cable transmissions.*

BODY-9   *The third and outer cover was addressed to the open head of the mission; in an embassy this would be the ambassador. The envelopes were sealed in five places, one seal in the middle and one at each corner. The message was then taken by the officer responsible for it in person to the dispatch room. There it was handed to a courier responsible for taking it to the Foreign Office (Ministry of Foreign Affairs). The courier, according to Akhmedov, was invariably a "GPU man."*

BODY-10   *"Several sources have stated that Soviet couriers are armed while accompanying mail."*

BODY-11   *"Soviet couriers entering and leaving the United States since the end of World War II have traveled mainly by air. Only when accompanying very bulky mail would other passage be likely. They are met at the airport by a car from the local Soviet mission and by one or more representatives of the mission."*

BODY-12   *From several sources there is information that Soviet diplomatic pouches, during the 1930's at least, were equipped with incendiary devices which could be set off instantly by the courier in an emergency.*

BODY-13   *The suite is subdivided into an outer and an inner section, in some instances, by steel doors. The outer rooms are reading rooms where authorized personnel may review secret communications directed to their attention. The inner rooms are reserved for cipher clerks and their organizational superiors. The windows in this section are equipped with iron bars and steel shutters. Each secret section is provided with an incinerator for burning secret papers, and the suite is partially fireproofed with sheet metal facings on the inner sides of nonfireproof doors. Sources also agree that firearms are maintained within the secret section for use in an emergency.*

BODY-14   *He said these papers were burned on the floor of the secret section. Benzine and other inflammable material, maintained for that purpose in the secret section, were used to hasten the burning.*

BODY-15   *Each service was furnished its own code and cipher system, and access to it was limited to the clerks and their service chiefs. The chief of the secret section was responsible for security within the unit, for coordinating the incoming and outgoing communications, and for maintaining the secret files and papers.*

BODY-16   *It would also seem that this key post would be one sought after by the MGB representation in keeping with its security responsibilities in a mission abroad.*

BODY-18   "Living accommodations, frequently are provided for the secret section personnel on embassy or consulate premises. Sources familiar with the habits of secret section workers in Soviet establishments in the United States agree that their outside contacts are severely restricted."

BODY-19   The conversion of the original Russian words of a message into the final cipher text of numerals in groups of five digits is a process which is outside the scope of this study. It may be described briefly, however, as a two-step operation. In the first stage, Russian plain-text words are converted into five-digit groups by reference to a code book. This code book consists of a list of alphabetically arranged words and phrases together with five-digit equivalents for each word and phrase. The second stage, or final step, involves the use of a sheet of random five-digit numbers which are added to the numbers obtained from the code book.

BODY-21   "A study of Soviet intelligence communications would be incomplete without comment on the use of microphotography. Thirty-five mm. undeveloped film is almost universally used in Soviet operations to convey documentary intelligence to the 'Centre.' It has been noted in the foregoing that material qualifying as to brevity and urgency may be dispatched by cable. However, in certain lines of operation, for example in the field of technical and scientific development, it is necessary for the intelligence services to obtain complete documents for the accomplishment of their missions."

BODY-22   "In some instances the source-agent with access to sought-after documents is trained and equipped for this work. For example, and it is only one of many which might be selected, Andrei Schevchenko, a Soviet official on the Amtorg staff in New York City, in 1945, attempted to penetrate the secret library of an American aircraft manufacturer."

BODY-23   "In the interest of security and space, bulky material can be copied upon reaching there and transmitted as undeveloped film by courier."

BODY-24   "It would serve no purpose to recount the many instances in Soviet operations in the United States in which microphotography has been employed. It is characteristic of nearly all of them."

BODY-25   The present study indicates that Soviet operations, under strictly clandestine conditions, have relied on agent radio for the main link between networks and the USSR, augmenting this main channel with courier and mail traffic. However, it should be noted that courier and mail links are less likely to connect a network with the USSR than with an open Soviet establishment in the same or a nearby country.

BODY-26   The late Walter Krivitsky, a Soviet intelligence official until his defection in 1937, stated that the Soviet Military Intelligence service began organizing a courier system among seamen in 1926, with Hamburg the center of this activity. About 200 seamen on ships between German and American ports were enlisted. The system was still functioning in 1937, but Krivitsky felt it was being used only to test its efficiency in the event war interrupted other channels.

BODY-27   "However, several operations in Latin America, during the late 1930's and early 1940's, were linked with open Soviet channels in the United States and were directed by Soviet officials in this country. Clandestine couriers and a system of mail drops for enciphered secret writing messages were employed."

BODY-28   "Beginning in the same month, and closely conforming with the schedule given in the letter, a station in New York, believed to have been located in the Soviet Consulate there, made repeated attempts to contact the Buenos Aires station. This station used the same cipher as the letter of February 1, 1943."

BODY-31　Klausen's 100 watt equipment was estimated to have been capable of a 1200-mile range.

BODY-32　"In his personal conduct, his rule was: 'to act cheerful before others, to look stupid, and especially to make it known I was interested in amateur radio.' He hired his domestic help for day service only. He dismantled and concealed his equipment when it was not in use (in a wardrobe trunk), estimating that he could assemble and be in operation in ten minutes and dismantle in five minutes."

BODY-33　Contrary to Sorge's belief, however, many other Soviet operations have disclosed that radio operators more often than not do their own cipher work.

BODY-34　Japanese police officials commented that the code system employed by the Sorge network was ideal from the standpoint of security. The cipher was difficult to read because of the rare recurrence of the same symbols due to the use of the "German Statistical Yearbook." It was stated that normally, when an additive table is employed, its length is limited, but this book offered "an almost infinite variety of figures." The code key was easily memorizable by the average person; and, "as long as the user took care to remove coded messages from his person and to burn all evidence immediately after transmission," the Japanese authorities felt that a house search would have been unproductive.

BODY-35　"Notwithstanding the earlier comment made by Klausen that he did not stay on the air for a long period, he elsewhere stated he often worked in a four-hour stretch."

BODY-36　Recognizing that all the facts are not available, it seems to be correct to say that a number of very effective Soviet networks capable of developing intelligence of high value to the Soviet Union were, by 1943, either eliminated or cut off by communications breakdowns.

BODY-37　"In spite of the presence of Soviet official representation in Germany up to the date of the invasion of the Soviet Union, much of the Soviet intelligence activity against Germany after the Nazis suppressed the German Communist Party was directed from."

BODY-39　The first major break for the Germans was the uncovering of a station operated by the Trepper organization in Brussels in December, 1941. Several of the group were arrested, a complete photographic laboratory was seized, a quantity of counterfeit identity cards and a volume of plain-text and ciphered traffic confiscated. One of the principal agents, one Mavkarov, a trained Soviet radio technician, walked into the arms of the German police on the morning following the raid, when he appeared at the house, unaware of what had taken place, with a set of messages for transmission.

BODY-40　This enabled the Germans to decipher a quantity of back traffic and to uncover important network links inside Germany. One of the groups exposed was headed by Harro Schulze-Boysen, a Luftwaffe officer assigned to staff work in the German Air Ministry. Schulze-Boysen had liaison with an official of the Soviet Trade Delegation in Berlin until the mission was withdrawn in June, 1941. The Soviet official turned an agent radio over to him at that time, but technical difficulties prevented him from establishing contact with the "Centre." Late in 1941 one of the agents in the Trepper organization was dispatched from Brussels to contact Schulze-Boysen in Germany to assist in overcoming the technical difficulties, and to aid the

BODY-41　"All together, 80 persons were arrested, an indication that this was a major blow to Soviet intelligence."

BODY-42   "In neutral Switzerland, however, three agent radio stations, best known by the German code name 'Rote Drei,' served an important Soviet operation in a most effective way until late 1943. A German official has given the following account of the damage done to the German cause by this Soviet group."

BODY-43   "In the most critical period on the eastern front, at the time of the battles around Stalingrad and in the Caucasus, and then later in the spring, summer and autumn of 1943, in those decisive days when the German armies in the southern and central sectors of the eastern front were sweeping back, in those days when one expected that somewhere, perhaps on the Dneiper they would be able to make a stand, check the onrushing tide of the Russian armies, and build a new firm front, precisely in those days, weeks, and months the most secret information regarding the troop units, strength, assembly areas, intentions, etc. was passing currently through Switzerland to Moscow."

BODY-44   "Before this operation had progressed very far, Germany and Great Britain were at war, and Foote, using British documents, was hastily withdrawn from Germany. Foote then took an apartment in Lausanne, Switzerland, passing himself off as a 'leisure demigre Englishman.' He was given elementary instruction in radio operation and at length installed a transmitter in his apartment."

BODY-45   The urgency of the situation made it sometimes necessary to broadcast for hours at a time, in violation of security rules. In an enemy country, he felt, this would have led to early discovery, but in Switzerland appears not to have created much interest until later. Foote established contact with the Soviet control station through a fixed call signal on a fixed wave length. When the "Centre" replied to his signal, Foote then switched to his "working wave length." After establishing the initial contact, the "Centre" did the same. Foote felt this practice cut to a minimum the possibility of radio monitoring.

BODY-46   "The urgency of the situation seems to have compelled the use of Foote's station in spite of the obvious danger."

BODY-47   The surviving operations in Switzerland were thus cut off. These included the most valuable of all Soviet sources in wartime Germany, a source which has never been completely identified. The material, conceded to have come directly from the highest German military circles, was referred to as the 'Lucy" source, and was funneled through Rachel Duebendorfer to Rado. In November, 1943, Duebendorfer wrote an open code letter to an acquaintance in Montreal, Hermina Rabinowitch, the contents of which are revealed in the Report of the Royal Commission, with instructions to pass it along to the Soviet Embassy at Ottawa. Through this means, Duebendorfer attempted to re-establish contact with the "Centre." It must be

BODY-48   "The international situation might result in the withdrawal of official Soviet representatives in Sweden and make necessary the use of radio transmittal in sending data to the Soviet Union."

BODY-49   "His instructions were to check the cache on odd weekdays between 1:00 and 2:30 p.m. He never saw nor identified the courier who visited this drop. On even weekdays Katz was under instructions to pass a designated street corner at the same hour of the day in order that the network could have him observed and be assured that he was not under arrest."

BODY-50   In summing up this account of clandestine operations in Western Europe, it can be said that the services of many valuable sources and some entire networks were lost because they had to rely on agent radio, and in those areas in which the monitoring services were well developed, radio operations could not be concealed over an *extended period. The exceptional case was the group in Switzerland, where radio control seems to have been ineffective until 1943.*

BODY-51   *On the theory that direction-finding equipment could not be brought into and be in operation in an agent radio's immediate vicinity in less than one hour, these student agents were instructed to limit their transmissions to one hour or less.*

BODY-52   *Another Soviet innovation is the development of a more compact agent radio. During the latter part of World War II, and during the years since the war, a radio referred to as the "Tensor M" model has made its appearance in widely scattered Soviet operations. This model or variations of it were furnished behind-the-lines agents parachuted into Germany late in the war, and have been furnished agents in Japan, Finland, and Western Europe in more recent operations. This equipment consists of three, and sometimes four, units packaged separately (receivers, transmitters, and rectifiers) in metal cases, each unit of which measures approximately 1 1/2 by 4 by 7 inches.*

BODY-53   *Their construction indicates the units are factory produced, primarily for intelligence service use. Under good operating conditions this equipment is capable of transmitting -up to or exceeding 1000 miles. The "Tensor M" type equipment is more readily concealed and transported than the earlier Soviet agent-type radio, many of which were improvised and agent built.*

BODY-54   *"The radio equipment provided the agents in these operations was similar to the 'Tensor M' type described in the foregoing. In one case, the agents, secretly entering the country of operation, brought it in, in a small suitcase. In the other, the agent, on arriving in the country safely, transmitted an open code letter to a mail drop outside the country, and the radio was brought in by courier and turned over to him personally."*

BODY-55   *In order not to exceed the one-hour broadcast time, there was provision for a unilateral contact, to occur on a specified frequency at a given time on the night prior to the bilateral contact. Acknowledgment of the receipt of the unilateral message would, thus, be made by the receiving party during the subsequent bilateral session. Unilateral contacts, offering greater security from direction finding, increased in number, and the bilateral contacts decreased, as these operations progressed.*

BODY-56   *The cipher systems used in the operations in question conform generally to those described earlier in this paper. The plain text is converted into numbers, the key to which is in a memorized code word. In the second stage reference is made to a key book, and a second set of numbers is obtained. The two products are added, and the final cipher obtained. A variation of this system was used also in these operations, in which the numerals in the latter stage were then transposed into letters of the alphabet, and the message as transmitted is in letters rather than numbers.*

BODY-57   *"During the early period of the operations in question regular courier liaison, with personal meetings, occurred about once a month, later being reduced to three-month intervals. Such meetings were stipulated as to time, place, and recognition signals; and it was in this manner that funds and equipment were brought in to the operating group and the bulkier reports and documents were transmitted to the 'Centre.'"*

BODY-58   *He was given detailed instructions for locating a brick wall in which one brick was missing. By reaching deeply into this hole, the agent found the package.*

BODY-59   *"In the first house the tenants led the police immediately to the crypt; but in the other, although the station was in operation when the raid began, it was many hours before the raiding party located the crypt and then only with aid of mine-detecting equipment. A Greek Communist leader, in the crypt when it was located, shot and killed himself before the police gained entrance."*

BODY-60   *The most recent and the outstanding Soviet achievement in clandestine communications is the development of an automatic tape transmitter, capable of sending up to 500 words a minute, adapted for use in conjunction with the 'Tensor M""' type equipment. Such equipment, which will fit readily into a piece of luggage 18 inches in length, has been placed in use by Soviet intelligence.*

BODY-61   *"Akhmedov, to whom we have referred previously, has stated that the microdot process was known to the Fourth Department (Soviet Military Intelligence) in 1940, and related a specific instance of its use at that time. One Volnuchin was dispatched to the United States as a resident late in 1940, and was given a letter to deliver to the Military Attache at Washington. The cover text was in the form of a letter from a relative; the microdot was placed over an 'i.' Akhmedov recalled that Volnuchin lost the letter en route, and on reporting the fact was recalled from Washington and dismissed from the service."*

BODY-62   *"Lacking the speed of radio and the capacity of a courier system, secret ink communication might be looked upon as an auxiliary or emergency medium. Another form of written communication which must be considered, and which cannot be fully treated herein, is open code. This is a general term for the practice of concealing messages within innocuous appearing personal correspondence or other cover texts. Situations which have not been provided for occasion the use of double-meaning language, another form of open code, and for this reason it is of particular interest."*

BODY-63   *The reference in the second letter to 'Znamensky 19,' the Moscow headquarters address of the GRU, was considered particularly indiscreet by Soviet intelligence officials in Ottawa.*

BODY-64   *Under clandestine conditions, the future prospect would seem to be for heavier reliance upon agent radio if automatic transmitting equipment proves to be effective. Courier systems will be necessary to sustain operations over a long period of time, and the microdot and secret ink processes may in some instances replace the 35 mm. film in the hands of the courier.*

SOVIET INTELLIGENCE

COMMUNICATIONS

FEDERAL BUREAU OF INVESTIGATION
UNITED STATES DEPARTMENT OF JUSTICE
J. Edgar Hoover, Director

SOVIET INTELLIGENCE

COMMUNICATIONS

September 1952

FEDERAL BUREAU OF INVESTIGATION
UNITED STATES DEPARTMENT OF JUSTICE
J. Edgar Hoover, Director

TABLE OF CONTENTS

Page

Introduction

An ideal counterintelligence operation is the penetration of an adversary's communications between the service headquarters and the operating networks. It is this source which offers the most complete and most authentic account of the activities being conducted. It is necessary, therefore, that his communications procedures be understood, and it is with this purpose in mind that the present study of Soviet intelligence communications is undertaken.

It is being divided into two parts: (1) the open and ostensibly legal channels, as now available in the United States, through official Soviet missions; (2) the clandestine channels which would be necessary were the official delegations to be withdrawn from the United States. Internal communications within the various networks, always clandestine in nature, are not within the scope of this paper.

- i -

SOVIET INTELLIGENCE COMMUNICATIONS

I. OPEN CHANNELS

The term "open channels," as used herein, refers to: (1) enciphered cable and radio traffic transmitted through commercial facilities by Soviet trade and diplomatic establishments; (2) the Soviet diplomatic couriers. The first is used for brief and urgent messages; the latter for the main burden of intelligence traffic.

Although, properly, a distinction could be made, commercial cablegrams and radiograms will be considered as one medium and will be generally referred to as "cable" traffic.

Headquarters Communications Procedures

The procedures for handling secret communications at the Moscow headquarters of Soviet Military Intelligence (GRU), although somewhat dated, have been described by two reliable sources. Comparable information is not available concerning the handling of communications at the headquarters of the Foreign Directorate of the Ministry of State Security (MGB). However, the procedures would seem to be generally the same, being governed by prescribed rules for handling secret communications, which are in effect throughout the Soviet State apparatus. It might be noted, in this connection, that "secret sections" are established in all Soviet enterprises for the handling of secret papers and are said to function under regulations promulgated by the MGB. The secret section personnel, however, is recruited from the most trusted Party or Komsomol members in the particular enterprise and is not necessarily MGB personnel.

With respect to incoming and outgoing cable traffic, Ismail Akhmedov, formerly chief of an operating section in GRU headquarters in Moscow, has given the following account of the procedure in effect there during his tenure, 1940 and 1941:

All outgoing communications prepared by him or his subordinates were drafted personally and by hand and were passed by hand to the chief of the code section. This latter section was in a walled-off portion of the headquarters building, accessible only through a locked and guarded fireproof door, admission to which was restricted to the chief of GRU or his immediate assistant and code section personnel. After being enciphered, the messages were transmitted from there to the cable facilities. A more complete supplement,

- 2 -

in many instances, was then prepared and transmitted by the diplomatic pouch.

Similarly, incoming messages were received in the code section, were deciphered, and distributed by the chief of the code section to the various chiefs of the operating sections. All messages sent to and received from a resident abroad were filed in that resident's dossier.

Igor Gouzenko served for a year as a cipher clerk in the secret cipher section at GRU headquarters in Moscow prior to his assignment in June, 1943, as cipher clerk for a Military Intelligence network in Ottawa. He stated there were about 150 cipher clerks in the cipher section at that time, with each clerk handling up to 3000 groups (i.e., groups of five figures) per day. Gouzenko estimated the messages averaged from 150 to 200 groups each, indicating about 3000 messages incoming and outgoing daily at that communications center. The serial numbers appearing on messages from the "Centre" to the chief of the network in Ottawa, as set forth in the Report of the Royal Commission, ranged from Number 10,458 on July 30, 1945, to Number 11,955 on August 22, 1945. This would indicate about 1500 cable dispatches emanating from GRU headquarters to operations

- 3 -

abroad in less than a month and is probably a more accurate figure than the former estimate.

The numbers in sequence on messages from the network in Ottawa to the "Centre" ranged from 209 on July 12, 1945, to 275 on August 30, 1945, or 65 cable dispatches to Moscow in the intervening 50 days.

These figures give a glimpse of the extent to which Soviet intelligence operations abroad rely upon enciphered cable transmissions.

It might be noted here that Soviet establishments in the Far East and in several of the European countries instead of using commercial facilities have made use of their own radiotelegraphy hookup with Moscow. This practice, which seems to have been dictated by geographical considerations and cost factors, has not been the rule in Soviet operations in the United States. Although the former Soviet consulates in New York and San Francisco were equipped with radio stations, their known use for intelligence purposes was limited to one series of clandestine communications. This will be described in a subsequent portion of this study.

- 4 -

With respect to mail to be transmitted via the diplomatic pouch, Akhmedov gave the following account:

Such mail was sent under a triple cover. The innermost cover bore the name of the resident (i.e., a GRU officer) for whom the message was intended. The second cover bore a code name indicating the mission official responsible for passing the communication. (It will be seen in the following pages that this is probably the chief of the mission's secret cipher section.) The third and outer cover was addressed to the open head of the mission; in an embassy this would be the ambassador. The envelopes were sealed in five places, one seal in the middle and one at each corner.

The message was then taken by the officer responsible for it in person to the dispatch room. There it was handed to a courier responsible for taking it to the Foreign Office (Ministry of Foreign Affairs). The courier, according to Akhmedov, was invariably a "GPU man." Elsewhere, this source has stated that diplomatic couriers were selected from both GPU (later NKVD and currently MGB) personnel and Soviet Military Intelligence (now GRU) personnel, although preponderantly from the former.

- 5 -

The question arises as to whether all mail sent by the diplomatic pouch is enciphered. In this connection, Gouzenko has stated that only that portion which identifies agents, places of meetings, addresses, telephone numbers, and other compromising detail is enciphered, but he did not indicate whether a light or heavy cipher was used.

Diplomatic Couriers

As noted in the foregoing, Akhmedov commented that the diplomatic couriers are selected from GPU (now MGB) and GRU personnel. He said these selections were made with the approval of Georgi Malenkov of the Politburo. When they are assigned as couriers, they are under the supervision of the Foreign Office.

Akhmedov and other sources have stated that couriers usually travel in pairs when accompanying mail. Sources familiar with the habits and movements of Soviet couriers in the United States have corroborated this. While traveling, they eat and sleep in shifts and, wherever possible, obtain closed compartments. Several sources have stated that Soviet couriers are armed while accompanying mail.

- 6 -

It might also be noted that a Soviet courier assignment is regarded as most desirable duty, and many have strong personal connections with high Soviet officials.

Soviet couriers entering and leaving the United States since the end of World War II have traveled mainly by air. Only when accompanying very bulky mail would other passage be likely. They are met at the airport by a car from the local Soviet mission and by one or more representatives of the mission. Logically, the latter would be connected with the secret cipher section, which will be described in the following pages. On their departure, the couriers are accompanied to the airport in a Soviet car.

The couriers' baggage frequently consists of several pieces: suitcases, brief cases, boxes tied with rope, and canvas pouches. The most secret mail, it appears, is carried in the pouches, which are reported to contain special compartments for the intelligence services' 35 mm. film. The descriptions of the Soviet pouches have varied. One reliable source states that many are 10 to 12 by 18 to 20 inches, bearing wax seals and metal fasteners, and frequently are tied with cord. Others have described them as up to 28 inches in length and leather-reinforced.

- 7 -

From several sources there is information that Soviet diplomatic pouches, during the 1930's at least, were equipped with incendiary devices which could be set off instantly by the courier in an emergency. In one account the source said the pouch was built with a shallow compartment across the bottom which was filled with a highly combustible chemical. A cord extended from this compartment up the inside of the pouch and out the top where it could be reached without opening the pouch. This connected with a detonating device for igniting the chemical and thus destroying the pouch and contents.

Secret Section Facilities Abroad

One section of each Soviet consulate, embassy, or commercial establishment abroad is set aside for the processing of secret communications and the maintenance of secret files. Incoming messages are received there, and outgoing messages to be transmitted by cable or pouch are handled in that section, which is referred to as the "secret section" or "secret division." The following is a composite description of such facilities received from a number of reliable sources:

- 8 -

This suite of rooms, described by some sources as vault type, is separated from the rest of the establishment by steel doors which lock from within. One or more members of the secret section staff are in constant attendance. To gain entrance it is necessary to summon an attendant by pressing a bell or buzzer. The suite is subdivided into an outer and an inner section, in some instances, by steel doors. The outer rooms are reading rooms where authorized personnel may review secret communications directed to their attention. The inner rooms are reserved for cipher clerks and their organizational superiors. The windows in this section are equipped with iron bars and steel shutters. Each secret section is provided with an incinerator for burning secret papers, and the suite is partially fireproofed with sheet metal facings on the inner sides of nonfireproof doors.

Sources also agree that firearms are maintained within the secret section for use in an emergency.

Akhmedov, referred to in the foregoing, was assigned to the Soviet Embassy in Berlin on June 22, 1941, when Germany invaded the Soviet Union. He states he personally assisted in burning secret papers in the secret section of the embassy, even while

- 9 -

the German police were attempting to gain entrance. He said these papers were burned on the floor of the secret section. Benzine and other inflammable material, maintained for that purpose in the secret section, were used to hasten the burning.

Operation of the Secret Cipher Section

The best available information concerning the secret cipher sections in Soviet establishments abroad seems to be that furnished by Igor Gouzenko on the unit in the Soviet Embassy in Ottawa. This can be augmented somewhat by other sources, generally in agreement.

The secret cipher section in Ottawa was located in one wing of the building, isolated from the remainder of the offices by steel doors, and was accessible to cipher personnel and to the ranking service officials in the Embassy. It consisted of eight rooms, seven of which were assigned to the various cipher clerks. The eighth served as a central message center and secret file room. Only the chief of the secret section was permitted regular access to the latter room.

- 10 -

Five separate services were represented on the cipher staff. Each service worked independently of other services within the unit and under the direction of his service superior. Thus, the Foreign Office clerks worked under the Ambassador, the Ministry of Foreign Trade clerks worked under the Commercial Secretary, a clerk was designated to handle the communications of the Communist Party representative in the Embassy, and cipher clerks were assigned to the then NKVD resident chief and the Military Intelligence resident chief. This latter position was the one held by Gouzenko, working under the Military Attache.

Each service was furnished its own code and cipher system, and access to it was limited to the clerks and their service chiefs.

The chief of the secret section was responsible for security within the unit, for coordinating the incoming and outgoing communications, and for maintaining the secret files and papers. While it is indicated that the chief of the secret section in Ottawa had no cryptographic duties, sources familiar with other Soviet installations indicate that one of the cryptographic employees is designated

- 11 -

as the chief, which duties are supplementary to his regular work. It would also seem that this key post would be one sought after by the MGB representation in keeping with its security responsibilities in a mission abroad. *

The incoming secret communications, received by cable and pouch, were delivered to the chief of the secret section (another source stated that all mail is delivered to the chief of the secret section); it was his responsibility to sort the communications and deliver them to the proper officials. The chief collected the outgoing communications, both cable and pouch messages, and was responsible for their dispatch. In this way outgoing cable dispatches emanated from the same person and bore no readily distinguishable characteristics, whether they were regular Foreign Office or intelligence traffic.

Similarly, the chief made up the outgoing pouches and turned them over to the couriers.

The chief of the secret section in Ottawa was responsible for maintaining the central safe and secret file room. A clerk

---

* It has been asserted that the secret sections are operated under the supervision of MGB. This is not taken as necessarily correct, although it is probably true that some chiefs of secret section have MGB connections.

- 12 -

was required to place his code books, cipher pads, and clear text messages in a pouch which he sealed with his own wax impression when they were not in use. The pouch was then turned over to the chief, who placed it in the central safe.

A similar arrangement was in effect in the Soviet Embassy in Berlin, according to Ismail Akhmedov, in June, 1941. He said the secret section included an inner room which was accessible only to the ambassador, the chief resident of NKVD, the cipher men, and the wireless operators. Some of the cipher men were sometimes excluded from the inner room. This room contained a single safe. The chiefs of the intelligence services maintained pouch-type bags in which were placed the working materials, which were sealed and delivered to the cipher man having custody of the safe. Such pouches were duly registered and placed in the safe.

In Ottawa Gouzenko maintained a safe in his own cipher room for the Military Attache, in which he was permitted to retain reports on agent networks, notes on contacts with agents, the Military Attache's diary, and other operational and administrative papers. Clear text copies of enciphered or deciphered communications between Ottawa and Moscow were, as we have noted in the foregoing, placed

- 13 -

in the pouch and deposited in the central safe. These were filed in numerical sequence, with a new series beginning the first day of each year.

Although Gouzenko was the only cipher clerk assigned to the Military Attache in Ottawa, it might be of interest to note that he learned from one of his associates that the Soviet Military Attache in Washington, during the same period, had five cipher clerks assigned to handle intelligence traffic.

Secret Section Personnel

Several Soviet defector sources have referred to the restrictions imposed upon the secret section staff in their social activity. They are ordinarily not permitted to have any contact with persons outside the Soviet staff, and fraternization with nonsecret section Soviet personnel is not encouraged. Living accommodations frequently are provided for the secret section personnel on embassy or consulate premises. Sources familiar with the habits of secret section workers in Soviet establishments in the United States agree that their outside contacts are severely restricted. One such employee has indicated he is not permitted on the streets after 10:00 p.m.

- 14 -

Cipher Pads and Code Books

The Soviet intelligence communications transmitted via commercial facilities are, of course, tightly enciphered. The conversion of the original Russian words of a message into the final cipher text of numerals in groups of five digits is a process which is outside the scope of this study. It may be described briefly, however, as a two-step operation. In the first stage, Russian plain-text words are converted into five-digit groups by reference to a code book. This code book consists of a list of alphabetically arranged words and phrases together with five-digit equivalents for each word and phrase. The second stage, or final step, involves the use of a sheet of random five-digit numbers which are added to the numbers obtained from the code book. These sheets of additive keys are removed from a pad and are used one time only. Thus there are two instruments necessary for effecting a coded message, a code book and a cipher pad.

Sources familiar with Soviet intelligence procedures are in agreement that the code books are changed perhaps at six-month to one-year intervals. The code books used by Igor Gouzenko in Ottawa were bound in a blue cover and were about six by nine inches

- 15 -

in size. The outer cover bore the Russian equivalent of "Secret" in the upper right-hand corner, and the equivalent of "Copy Number___" in the same location. In the center of the cover appeared the equivalent of "Code" followed by letter and number. (Thus: "Code A-22") Two pages of the code books contained instructions on its use.

The cipher pads are furnished to the intelligence services abroad at much more frequent intervals. One source estimated that new pads would arrive about every two weeks. Each sheet of the pad is used once and then destroyed, hence the term "one-time pad." The pads used by Gouzenko bore the seal of the People's Commissariat of Defense, then the body to which the Soviet Army, and thus the Military Attache, was ultimately responsible. Gouzenko described the pads as follows:

> Each branch of the service had its own seal and all were different. The pad is bound in celluloid, with the binding lace going through brass eyelets in the celluloid. The top celluloid binding is a strip around the pad. ... The bottom celluloid binding is solid and bears the word "Inflammable" printed thereon.

> The ends of the binding lace are brought to the top cover and the seal is placed over the ends (of the lace). Underneath the top cover are two sheets of black paper which must be removed before using the pad. The numbers are arranged in horizontal rows of 5 in each row, with 10 rows to the page.

- 16 -

Gouzenko diagramed a cipher pad on a scale of 3 1/2 by 4 1/2 inches. This may or may not be its true size, since he did not indicate thereon. However, another Soviet defector, referring to the "one-time cipher pack" in use by the Soviets in 1940, said they were contained in grey or white sealed envelopes, about four by five inches, which bore five seals stamped in red sealing wax. This source said the envelope contained a number of very thin slips of paper separated by black paper. Each slip contained the cipher numbers to be used on a particular date.

Microphotography

A study of Soviet intelligence communications would be incomplete without comment on the use of microphotography. Thirty-five mm. undeveloped film is almost universally used in Soviet operations to convey documentary intelligence to the "Centre." It has been noted in the foregoing that material qualifying as to brevity and urgency may be dispatched by cable. However, in certain lines of operation, for example in the field of technical and scientific development, it is necessary for the intelligence services to obtain complete documents for the accomplishment of their missions. There

- 17 -

is an obvious advantage in submitting a complete document rather than an intelligence agent's uninformed version of its contents. Copying such documents on 35 mm. film is practical from the standpoint of security and space. Therefore, we can look for this process at one stage or another in an operation.

In some instances the source-agent with access to sought-after documents is trained and equipped for this work. For example, and it is only one of many which might be selected, Andrei Schevchenko, a Soviet official on the Amtorg staff in New York City, in 1945, attempted to penetrate the secret library of an American aircraft manufacturer. After the build-up process, in which Schevchenko felt he had gotten a measure of control over the source, he produced a Zeiss Ikon camera, giving it to the source together with instructions in document photography. He later tried to get the camera back when the source failed to produce the desired results. For a time, however, the source, under FBI control, turned over to him information cleared for the purpose on rolls of film. At one point the source told Schevchenko he would like to learn to develop the film himself, but the latter insisted he wanted only undeveloped film. This, of course,

- 18 -

is a security precaution. If the container were opened other than in a darkroom, the film would be ruined and evidence destroyed.

Another security note, in this connection, is in the fact that Schevchenko excused himself immediately after the delivery of film was made to him on the pretext that he had to meet another person. Later he returned to the source, giving him further lengthy instructions on the use of the camera. Presumably he wanted to get rid of the film as quickly as possible, undeveloped or not.

Any open Soviet establishment will, of course, be equipped for document photography; and, in the interest of security and space, bulky material can be copied upon reaching there and transmitted as undeveloped film by courier.

The photography also might be handled on an intermediate level, between the source and the Soviet establishment. There are numerous instances available from Soviet operations in the United States of this practice. For example, the Ovakimian network, during the mid-1930's, maintained cover apartments in New York for this purpose. Of more recent date the Julius Rosenberg group maintained cover apartments equipped with photographic laboratories. A complete laboratory was maintained by Nathan Gregory

- 19 -

Silvermaster in the basement of his own residence in Washington, D. C., where, according to Elizabeth Bentley, he and his associate, Ludwig Ullman, photographed documents which they obtained temporarily. It would serve no purpose to recount the many instances in Soviet operations in the United States in which microphotography has been employed. It is characteristic of nearly all of them. The Leica camera, or similar 35 mm. models, will usually be found in the paraphernalia of a Soviet career agent.

* * * * * *

The foregoing outlines the communications mediums available to the Soviet networks operating at the present time in the United States. Were the various Soviet missions to be withdrawn, the networks remaining in operation would be required to employ clandestine facilities, inferior as to security and capacity.

- 20 -

II. CLANDESTINE COMMUNICATIONS

Three mediums are usually suggested when clandestine intelligence communications are being considered: agent radio, courier, and mail. The latter term includes "microdots," secret writing or open code letters directed to designated mail drops.

The present study indicates that Soviet operations, under strictly clandestine conditions, have relied upon agent radio (i.e., wireless telegraphy) for the main link between networks and the USSR, augmenting this main channel with courier and mail traffic. However, it should be noted that courier and mail links are less likely to connect a network with the USSR than with an open Soviet establishment in the same or a nearby country.

Clandestine Communications in the United States

The early Soviet intelligence operations in the United States were sustained largely by clandestine courier communications. During the late 1920's and the very early 1930's, seamen, particularly on ships between Hamburg, Germany, and New York,

- 21 -

were used as couriers by the networks headed by Alfred Tiltin, Moische Stern, and others. Funds for the networks were supplied through this medium and the intelligence production, much of it on 35 mm. film, was transmitted through this channel. Whittaker Chambers, Robert Gordon Switz, Nicholas Dozenberg, and others connected with these early Soviet networks have described the seamen-courier system.

The late Walter Krivitsky, a Soviet intelligence official until his defection in 1937, stated that the Soviet Military Intelligence service began organizing a courier system among seamen in 1926, with Hamburg the center of this activity. About 200 seamen on ships between German and American ports were enlisted. The system was still functioning in 1937, but Krivitsky felt it was being used only to test its efficiency in the event war interrupted other channels.

Following the establishment of diplomatic relations between the United States and the USSR in 1933, the need for such channels became less urgent; and in this country in recent years clandestine mediums have been relatively unknown in Soviet communications--excepting, of course, internal communications within

- 22 -

networks. However, several operations in Latin America, during the late 1930's and early 1940's, were linked with open Soviet channels in the United States and were directed by Soviet officials in this country. Clandestine couriers and a system of mail drops for enciphered secret writing messages were employed.

A series of letters between New York and Buenos Aires, and New York and Mexico City, intercepted by censorship beginning late in 1941 and continuing into 1943, were found to contain enciphered messages. The Mexico City letters, relating to Soviet intelligence efforts to free Frank Jacson, Trotsky's assassin, from prison, indicated many of the message series were not getting through on schedule to the mail addresses. Perhaps for this reason, a New York school teacher, Anna Vogel Colloms, in August, 1943, was dispatched to Mexico City as a courier. A box of blank stationery taken from her possession at a Texas border station revealed several pages of invisible writing in cipher.

The secret writing letters between Buenos Aires and New York concerned, in part, the establishment of a radio link between the two cities.

One of the letters, postmarked in New York, February 1,

- 23 -

1943, set up a schedule of call letters and broadcast times between two clandestine radio stations, one located in the New York area and one located in the Buenos Aires area. Beginning in the same month, and closely conforming with the schedule given in the letter, a station in New York, believed to have been located in the Soviet Consulate there, made repeated attempts to contact the Buenos Aires station. This station used the same cipher as the letter of February 1, 1943. The traffic was discontinued in October, 1943, by which time, or shortly thereafter, several South American countries had received Soviet trade or diplomatic missions. Thus, official channels may have been made available to the network in question.

Soviet networks in other parts of the world, however, have found it necessary to use clandestine channels to a large degree, and it might be useful to study some of the more important operations from a communications standpoint.

Sorge Network

Richard Sorge was assigned to Tokyo in 1935 on an undercover mission for the "Fourth Department," as Soviet Military Intelligence was then known. He was a German Communist who

- 24 -

entered the service of the Comintern during the late 1920's. Later he transferred to the intelligence service. He had an established reputation as a journalist, succeeded in submerging his Communist history, represented a reputable German newspaper in Tokyo, and gained complete acceptance in German official and social circles there. With such cover Sorge operated as remotely as possible from Soviet official channels. It was not until 1940 that he was given liaison with the Russian delegation in Tokyo, and this was at his request.

Several times a year members of the Sorge network were dispatched as couriers with rolls of 35 mm. film to either Hong Kong or Shanghai, where they met Moscow couriers. Arrangements for such contact had been made by Sorge's radio station. In addition to delivering the film (Sorge sometimes accumulated 25 to 30 rolls between deliveries), the couriers returned with funds for Sorge's operation.

By 1940 travel into and out of Japan had come under more strict control, and Sorge had difficulty in safely passing his couriers through to China. For this reason he asked Moscow for liaison in Tokyo; and Moscow approved, although with some reluctance. Periodic meetings, participated in by Sorge, or one of his

- 25 -

group, and officials of the Soviet delegation in Tokyo (unknown to Sorge et al, but identified from photographs of Soviet personnel in the possession of the Japanese police) then began, with characteristic recognition signals and clandestine rendezvous. After this liaison was established, Sorge's microfilm reports to the "Centre" were passed on through this medium, and funds for the network were received in the same way. Such meetings were, however, set up through Sorge's radio communication system.

In October, 1941, Sorge, his radio operator, Max Klausen, and the remainder of the network were arrested by the Japanese police. The details of Sorge's operation, disclosed in a Japanese police report, have subsequently been made available. Portions of this account dealing with the radio operation are selected here to illustrate the technique involved.

Max Klausen, also a German Communist, was trained as a radio technician in the Soviet Union and was assigned to Sorge's network in Japan in 1935. Klausen used a commercial cover. At first he engaged in an export business, dealing in general merchandise. Later he was established in a small manufacturing business. Like Sorge, he successfully concealed from the German community

- 26 -

in Tokyo his Communist background and was completely accepted in it.

Klausen assembled his first transmitter and receiver shortly after his arrival in Japan from parts which he purchased in Tokyo, except for a telegraph key which he brought with him. He later built other units and seems to have been pleased with the fact that they were compact enough to fit into two suitcases, in which he carried them to and from his various broadcasting locations. More current Soviet radio equipment is, as will be seen in a later portion of this study, more compact in construction.

Klausen alternated between his own residence and the residences of other members of the network for his radio operation. These locations were selected with the following considerations in mind: (1) an upper floor for elevation; (2) a wooden frame dwelling to allow better transmission and reception; and (3) a densely populated area to make direction finding more difficult.

Klausen's 100 watt equipment was estimated to have been capable of a 1200-mile range. He believed that his control station was in Eastern Siberia, possibly Vladivostok, Komsomolsk, or Khabarovsk; but he had no certain knowledge of its location. The

- 27 -

Japanese Communications Ministry, on the other hand, believed the control station was in the direction of Shanghai, at least until 1940. In this connection, it appears that the Japanese police picked up signals from Klausen's station over an extended period but were not successful in locating the station or in deciphering the messages until leads from other sources led them to Klausen.

Although he was aware of the effectiveness of mobile direction finders, Klausen seems to have been confident that the Japanese police had not developed this technique; he said he assumed his broadcasts were monitored but felt he would not be traced closer than a "few kilometers." He alternated his location, avoided long periods of transmission, altered wave lengths and call letters, and was careful of outsiders. In his personal conduct, his rule was: "to act cheerful before others, to look stupid, and especially to make it known I was interested in amateur radio." He hired his domestic help for day service only. He dismantled and concealed his equipment when it was not in use (in a wardrobe trunk), estimating that he could assemble and be in operation in ten minutes and dismantle in five minutes. He avoided an outside antenna, stringing twin-braided copper wire about 25 feet long inside the room.

- 28 -

Klausen was not entrusted with the cipher until 1938. The outgoing communications were enciphered by Sorge and handed to Klausen. The incoming messages were handed to Sorge still in their cipher. Sorge said he obtained special permission from Moscow to teach Klausen the cipher in 1938 in order to relieve himself of the burden, but felt that this was an exception to the rule that the cipher "was revealed only to the head of a network." Contrary to Sorge's belief, however, many other Soviet operations have disclosed that radio operators more often than not do their own cipher work.

There is no indication that Sorge and Klausen restricted their contacts with each other. Incoming and outgoing messages were exchanged at meetings in restaurants and other public meeting places. On other occasions they openly visited each other's home.

The basic cipher key employed by Sorge and Klausen, by which one and two-digit numbers were substituted for individual letters of the alphabet, was memorized. This constituted the first step in the enciphering operation. A second step, introduced to make the cipher more secure, consisted of adding numbers to the basic cipher key numbers. The numbers used for adding were obtained

- 29 -

from tables appearing in the "German Statistical Yearbook," a book which was in keeping with their cover. The message itself contained an indicator group, giving the receiver the page and column of figures being used. Ordinary messages from the Soviet station were signed "Dal" (Russian equivalent for "Far East"), and this was later changed to "Organizer." Messages signed "Director" were either major directives, issued by the chief of Military Intelligence in Moscow, and recognized as such by Sorge, or special congratulatory or anniversary greetings.

Japanese police officials commented that the code system employed by the Sorge network was ideal from the standpoint of security. The cipher was difficult to read because of the rare recurrence of the same symbols due to the use of the "German Statistical Yearbook." It was stated that normally, when an additive table is employed, its length is limited, but this book offered "an almost infinite variety of figures." The code key was easily memorizable by the average person; and, "as long as the user took care to remove coded messages from his person and to burn all evidence immediately after transmission," the Japanese authorities felt that a house search would have been unproductive.

- 30 -

Until the "Chinese Incident" (1937) when the volume of traffic was relatively small, all radio contact was initiated by the control station. In each incoming message the time and date for the next contact would be stated. During this period contact was had at least once a week. Beginning in August, 1938, Sorge was notified that the Soviet station would stand by for calls from him during the first fifteen minutes of every hour. Klausen found that daybreak and sunset hours were best for transmission, but he most frequently operated during the 4:00 p.m. to 7:00 p.m. period. Notwithstanding the earlier comment made by Klausen that he did not stay on the air for a long period, he elsewhere stated he often worked in a four-hour stretch.

Klausen went on the air 60 times during 1939, dispatching about 23,000 words. About the same volume was handled in 1940. During the nine months the station operated in 1941, he broadcast about 20 times and dispatched about 13,000 words. Thus, in spite of liaison arrangements which Sorge was given in 1940, he continued to rely heavily on his agent radio.

After the outbreak of the Russo-German War, Sorge stated, he cut down on long reports and bulky documents and

- 31 -

concentrated on reporting essential facts by radio.

Communications in Western Europe, World War II

A volume of material is available for the study of Soviet intelligence communications under strictly clandestine conditions in Western Europe during and in the period just prior to World War II. After June 21, 1941, when the German invasion of Russia was launched, the Soviet networks in Germany and Western Europe became heavily reliant upon secret agent radio. Much of the information concerning Soviet operations during the period comes from German counter-intelligence records, which are in some instances fairly complete and in others only fragmentary. Recognizing that all the facts are not available, it seems to be correct to say that a number of very effective Soviet networks capable of developing intelligence of high value to the Soviet Union were, by 1943, either eliminated or cut off by communications breakdowns. These breakdowns can be traced to German successes in locating agent transmitters, to effective house searches which produced information on the network structures and ciphers, and to German successes in eliciting cooperation from network members when taken into custody.

- 32 -

The Soviet intelligence services were not completely unprepared for the eventuality confronting them on June 21, 1941. Ismail Akhmedov, identified in the foregoing, said each resident of Military Intelligence abroad was equipped with his own wireless. These were 100 watt portable units for emergency use, in anticipation of wartime conditions.

A German intelligence report, dated just prior to the opening of hostilities between Russia and Germany, described Soviet efforts to establish "a chain of secret radio stations in Berlin, and other important cities of the Greater Reich," as "almost provocative." These efforts were reported to have been headed by one Kobulov, the Soviet Embassy Counsellor, described as a "GPU" official. The same report also described the roundup of 60 persons in Czechoslovakia and the confiscation of a dozen secret radio stations during the same period.

In spite of the presence of Soviet official representation in Germany up to the date of the invasion of the Soviet Union, much of the Soviet intelligence activity against Germany after the Nazis suppressed the German Communist Party was directed from

- 33 -

the neighboring Low Countries and France. The resident directors of those operations relied upon the official Soviet channels until June, 1940, when they were disrupted by the German occupation.

A network headed by Leopold Trepper, established in Brussels under a commercial cover in 1938, maintained communications through the Soviet Trade Delegation in Brussels, until it was withdrawn in June, 1940. Trepper then moved to Paris and established contact with the Soviet Military Mission at Vichy, which, in turn, was withdrawn in June, 1941.

A branch of Trepper's organization, meanwhile, continued to function in Holland and Belgium. Dutch, Belgian, and exiled German Communists, together with several Soviet nationals (documented as Latin Americans, Finns, etc.), made up this group. An export-import company, with affiliated branches in Brussels and Paris, served as a cover for funds and communications and enabled the organization to continue and to expand contacts inside Germany.

After the German invasion of Russia the Trepper organization and the other Soviet networks in Western Europe were completely reliant upon agent radio for contact with the "Centre."

- 34 -

In those areas in which the German radio control organization could function such stations were rapidly silenced.

The first major break for the Germans was the uncovering of a station operated by the Trepper organization in Brussels in December, 1941. Several of the group were arrested, a complete photographic laboratory was seized, a quantity of counterfeit identity cards and a volume of plain-text and ciphered traffic confiscated. One of the principal agents, one Markarov, a trained Soviet radio technician, walked into the arms of the German police on the morning following the raid, when he appeared at the house, unaware of what had taken place, with a set of messages for transmission.

The remainder of Trepper's organization was then integrated with a group headed by Konstantine Jeffremov, a Soviet national who arrived in Brussels in 1939 undercover as a student of chemistry. Jeffremov was documented as a Finnish subject. He had taken over a group of German and Dutch Communists, and late in 1941 his group put an agent radio into operation. This station took over the Trepper communications with the "Centre," up to June, 1942, when it was located and confiscated by the German radio control organization.

- 35 -

Documents seized in this raid, together with the earlier seizure, enabled the Germans to fill out their knowledge of these Soviet operations to a large degree. Johann Wenzel, a German Communist long sought by the German police, was captured in this raid and under interrogation appears to have given away the cipher. This enabled the Germans to decipher a quantity of back traffic and to uncover important network links inside Germany.

One of the groups exposed was headed by Harro Schulze-Boysen, a Luftwaffe officer assigned to staff work in the German Air Ministry. Schulze-Boysen had liaison with an official of the Soviet Trade Delegation in Berlin until the mission was withdrawn in June, 1941. The Soviet official turned an agent radio over to him at that time, but technical difficulties prevented him from establishing contact with the "Centre." Late in 1941 one of the agents in the Trepper organization was dispatched from Brussels to contact Schulze-Boysen in Germany to assist in overcoming the technical difficulties, and to aid the group in getting into direct contact. This connection was exposed by the Brussels back traffic.

Another group, headed by Arvid Harnack, an employee of the German Ministry of Economics also was uncovered. Harnack

- 36 -

had been controlled by the same official of the Soviet Trade Delegation and also had been furnished an agent radio for direct contact with the "Centre." Liaison was arranged between the Schulze-Boysen and Harnack groups to provide each with an auxiliary communications channel. Meanwhile, neither group succeeded in making radio contact, and a courier link between Schulze-Boysen and Brussels and between Harnack and the Soviet Trade Delegation in Stockholm was maintained until late in the Summer of 1942 when both groups were eliminated. All together, 80 persons were arrested, an indication that this was a major blow to Soviet intelligence.

Ramifications of these Brussels seizures led to Holland, where several agent radios were silenced, only to be succeeded by others which had been held in reserve. When the reserve equipment was seized by the Germans, attempts were made to parachute agents and equipment into Holland. The same pattern was followed in Germany. In general, it might be said that the operations of the agent radios, if successful in making contact with the "Centre," were short-lived.

Meanwhile, Trepper and his organization in France made several attempts to establish radio communication with the

- 37 -

"Centre." Agent radios operated by the underground French Communist Party were placed at his disposal from time to time. All this activity came to an end late in 1942 when the German counterintelligence organization traced him through his business affiliation with the Brussels group, and uncovered his associates in Marseilles and Lyons.

In June, 1943, Trepper escaped from German custody, but he appears to have given the Germans a degree of cooperation and to have compromised several of his important associates before doing so.

German counterintelligence made a concerted effort to play back the agent radios uncovered in France and the Low Countries, setting up a special organization to coordinate and control the counteroperations. In some instances the original operators were at least partly cooperative. No great successes have been claimed for these attempts.

In neutral Switzerland, however, three agent radio stations, best known by the German code name "Rote Drei," served an important Soviet operation in a most effective way until late 1943. A German official has given the following account of the damage done to the German cause by this Soviet group:

- 38 -

"...in the most critical period on the eastern front, at the time of the battles around Stalingrad and in the Caucasus, and then later in the spring, summer and autumn of 1943, in those decisive days when the German armies in the southern and central sectors of the eastern front were sweeping back, in those days when one expected that somewhere, perhaps on the Dneiper they would be able to make a stand, check the onrushing tide of the Russian armies, and build a new firm front, precisely in those days, weeks, and months the most secret information regarding the troop units, strength, assembly areas, intentions, etc. was passing currently through Switzerland to Moscow. These were exclusively matters which must have come from the highest level of German military command."

The German monitoring service first intercepted the traffic between the "Rote Drei" stations in Switzerland and the control station in the USSR in June, 1941, and placed their position generally in the Lake Geneva region. They were quickly recognized as agent stations and henceforth were closely monitored. Not until 1944 was the cipher broken and the traffic read.

The principal figure in the "Rote Drei" group was Alexander Rado, an immigrant Hungarian cartographer. Prior to June, 1940, he maintained communication with Moscow via Paris, with microfilm couriers passing between his headquarters in Switzerland and Soviet official channels in France. The occupation of France by German troops suddenly cut this link, and it was necessary to integrate his network with another group operating in Switzerland

- 39 -

which had already succeeded in establishing radio communication with the "Centre." One of the stations made available to Rado was the one operated by Alexander Foote, who was recruited into Soviet intelligence when he returned to England in 1938 from service in the Loyalist Army in Spain. He was first assigned to establish himself as a resident in Munich, reporting out to a network superior in Geneva. Before this operation had progressed very far, Germany and Great Britain were at war, and Foote, using British documents, was hastily withdrawn from Germany.

Foote then took an apartment in Lausanne, Switzerland, passing himself off as a "leisured emigre Englishman." He was given elementary instruction in radio operation and at length installed a transmitter in his apartment. Foote's superior, a woman, also operated a unit in her residence near Geneva. This was later moved into Geneva and was operated by the proprietor of a radio repair shop. A third unit, operated by a Swiss woman Communist, who was trained by Foote, completed Rado's radio communications system.

Foote, who has written an account of his operations in Handbook for Spies, states that Rado's network consisted of some

- 40 -

60 sources, and after June, 1941, the three stations were fully oc-
cupied in carrying his traffic. The urgency of the situation made it
sometimes necessary to broadcast for hours at a time, in violation
of security rules. In an enemy country, he felt, this would have led
to early discovery, but in Switzerland appears not to have created
much interest until later.

Foote established contact with the Soviet control station
through a fixed call signal on a fixed wave length. When the "Centre"
replied to his signal, Foote then switched to his "working wave length."
After establishing the initial contact, the "Centre" did the same.
Foote felt this practice cut to a minimum the possibility of radio
monitoring.

All messages were enciphered in five-digit groups.
The first stage in the process was based on a memorized key for
converting the letters of the alphabet into numerals. In the second
stage—Foote calls it "closing the cipher"—a passage taken from a
text employed as a code book was also reduced to numbers, and the
latter product added to the product of the first stage. It is of interest
to note, as in the Sorge operation, Foote used a book dealing with
statistics for the second process. * Recognition groups inserted into

* Statistical Handbook of Foreign Trade, 1938, and
  Swiss Handbook of Trade Statistics, 1939

- 41 -

the ciphered text identified the page and passage used.

In 1943 the Swiss authorities became interested in the "Rote Drei" network. Foote was not immediately located, but his companion stations were identified and raided. In one of the raids copies of the plain-text messages, in some instances with an enciphered version attached, were found. This station was using Rado's personal cipher, thus compromising it. Foote, however, had his own cipher, and thus could continue to function; during the ensuing weeks his was the only link between the Rado organization and the "Centre." The urgency of the situation seems to have compelled the use of Foote's station in spite of the obvious danger.

A few weeks after the companion stations were raided, the Swiss police located Foote's transmitter. He had time to burn a few documents, and to put his set out of commission, before the police were able to break into his apartment. Subsequently, the Swiss attempted a play-back with this station, which failed, according to Foote, because Rado's cipher was used on the Foote unit. The Soviet station confirmed its suspicions by putting some "control questions" to the operators, who were unable to make the proper responses.

- 42 -

The surviving operations in Switzerland were thus cut off. These included the most valuable of all Soviet sources in wartime Germany, a source which has never been completely identified. The material, conceded to have come directly from the highest German military circles, was referred to as the "Lucy" source, and was funneled through Rachel Duebendorfer to Rado. In November, 1943, Duebendorfer wrote an open code letter to an acquaintance in Montreal, Hermina Rabinowitch, the contents of which are revealed in the Report of the Royal Commission, with instructions to pass it along to the Soviet Embassy at Ottawa. Through this means, Duebendorfer attempted to re-establish contact with the "Centre." It must be concluded that her situation was desperate to justify so evident a security breach.

Radio Operations in Sweden (1939-42)

The Swedish Radio Control Section, operating in conjunction with the counterintelligence police, located a number of clandestine agent radios being operated by Soviet intelligence during the 1939-1942 period. The networks for which the radio stations

- 43 -

were being operated were headed by Soviet officials on the staffs of the Soviet Legation, the Soviet Trade Commission, and the Soviet Travel Agency in Stockholm. One of these officials, Stefan Artemiev of the Soviet Legation, took the trouble to explain to one of his radio technicians that "the international situation might result in the with-drawal of official Soviet representatives in Sweden and make necessary the use of radio transmittal in sending data to the Soviet Union."

These cases seem to have been directed mainly toward information concerning German military movements in the Scandinavian peninsula and the Swedish military defenses. Some of the stations already were in contact with a control station located near Moscow, while others were in the process of establishing contact. The stations were located in private dwellings, many of them enlisting aid from Communist Party members and sympathizers.

One of the cases in this group, involving a youthful refugee named Lennart Katz, is of interest since it is an instance in which a radio operation was isolated from the remainder of network activities. Katz put a station into operation in June, 1942; it was located almost immediately and Katz was apprehended in the act of transmitting.

- 44 -

Katz, acting solely as a technician, neither enciphered nor deciphered. He received outgoing messages in cipher and delivered incoming ciphered messages at a cache in the remote countryside. His instructions were to check the cache on odd weekdays between 1:00 and 2:30 p.m. He never saw nor identified the courier who visited this drop. On even weekdays Katz was under instructions to pass a designated street corner at the same hour of the day in order that the network could have him observed and be assured that he was not under arrest.

This practice of using a cache as a liaison drop has been widely used by the Soviets in Europe and in recent years has been noted in connection with Russian operations in the United States. Further reference will be made to this device in a subsequent portion of this study.

In other cases in this Swedish group the radio technicians also performed cryptographic duties. It was observed that the key books used in such instances, which were popular editions of Swedish literature, could frequently be identified in house searches by their well-worn appearance. In one case the cryptographer customarily had dirty hands, and his code book was well smudged with finger impressions.

- 45 -

In summing up this account of clandestine operations in Western Europe, it can be said that the services of many valuable sources and some entire networks were lost because they had to rely on agent radio, and in those areas in which the monitoring services were well developed, radio operations could not be concealed over an extended period. The exceptional case was the group in Switzerland, where radio control seems to have been ineffective until 1943.

Postwar Developments in Clandestine Communications

There is in evidence a more thorough course of training, especially in agent radio technique, in the Soviet intelligence services. The curriculum of an eight-month training program offered prospective "illegal residents" of GRU in 1945 provided individual instruction and practice at various residential locations in and around Moscow, with no classroom work, for obvious security reasons.

Student agents were trained in the construction, repair, and operation of agent-type radio, and in Morse code, broadcasting technique, methods of camouflaging antennas, and in the

- 46 -

theory and practice of radio direction finding (goniometry).

Among the suggested measures for camouflaging antennas were the following: (1) stretch a third wire so it appears to be part of any exposed wires belonging to the electrical installation of a house; (2) simulate the installation of an electric wall plug for attaching an electric iron or table lamp, but using one of the terminals for the antenna; (3) form the antenna into a spiral and place it on the inside of a picture or mirror, using the end of the antenna to hang up the picture or mirror; (4) stretch the antenna on a balcony or in a court, so that it appears as a clothesline; and (5) install the antenna as though it were part of the usual house-type radio equipment.

On the theory that direction-finding equipment could not be brought into and be in operation in an agent radio's immediate vicinity in less than one hour, these student agents were instructed to limit their transmissions to one hour or less.

Places for concealment of equipment, when not in use, recommended in this GRU training course are not unusual: overstuffed furniture; false bottoms in wardrobes and other items of furniture; and secret compartments in the walls, ceilings and floors.

In addition to the course on radio operation, the prospective GRU "illegal residents" were given basic agent training in;

- 47 -

methods of security, forms of liaison (contacts, meets, etc.), re-
cruiting procedure, intelligence objectives, and enemy police organi-
zations and methods.

Document and nondocument photography and laboratory
work (using the 35 mm. Russian "Fed," a copy of the "Leica"),
cryptography, and the use of secret inks also were part of the course.

Another Soviet innovation is the development of a more
compact agent radio. During the latter part of World War II, and
during the years since the war, a radio referred to as the "Tensor M"
model has made its appearance in widely scattered Soviet operations.
This model or variations of it were furnished behind-the-lines agents
parachuted into Germany late in the war, and have been furnished
agents in Japan, Finland, and Western Europe in more recent operations.

This equipment consists of three, and sometimes
four, units packaged separately (receivers, transmitters, and
rectifiers) in metal cases, each unit of which measures approximately 1 1/2 by 4 by 7 inches. The complete set, with accessories,
can be fitted into a medium-sized piece of luggage. Although such
units have not been identified with anything produced in the English-
speaking countries, they bear, probably for reasons of deception,

- 48 -

English printing. Their construction indicates the units are factory produced, primarily for intelligence-service use. Under good operating conditions this equipment is capable of transmitting up to or exceeding 1000 miles.

The "Tensor M" type equipment is more readily concealed and transported than the earlier Soviet agent-type radio, many of which were improvised and agent built.

There is also an indication that the Soviets have developed a weather-resisting process permitting agent radio equipment to be buried in the ground for long periods of time. Such equipment is reported to have been furnished agents connected with a Soviet "stay behind" program in the satellite countries, who would be called into service should the Soviet Union lose control of that territory. The equipment is alleged to be buried in locations known only to the agent and his superior and is exhumed and examined once a year for defects. Meanwhile, the agent operators have been given cipher systems and call schedules and are held in readiness, with no other assignments.

Current Clandestine Operating Techniques

Two "illegal residences" in Western Europe, one of

- 49 -

which was established in 1948 and the other at an earlier date, operating under strictly clandestine circumstances, provide some fairly current information on Soviet methods. These operations were provided with two communications systems, agent radio and an overland courier link, connecting with an official Soviet mission in an adjoining country. First, the radio system will be described briefly.

The radio equipment provided the agents in these operations was similar to the "Tensor M" type described in the foregoing. In one case, the agents, secretly entering the country of operation, brought it in, in a small suitcase. In the other, the agent, on arriving in the country safely, transmitted an open code letter to a mail drop outside the country, and the radio was brought in by courier and turned over to him personally. Both units were set up and operated from private dwellings.

On their dispatch, these agents were provided with a schedule for several months in advance covering broadcast dates, times, and frequencies for communicating with the "Centre." (The control station is believed to have been located in or near Moscow.) This schedule, too complicated to be memorized, in one instance was photographed on silk and sewn into the lining of the agent's

- 50 -

clothing. The schedule had several provisions.

First, there was a table of bilateral contacts with the "Centre," each of which provided for two wave lengths, the first for regular contact, to be used during the first 15 minutes of the call, and the second, an alternate, to be used if the first did not result in contact.

In order not to exceed the one-hour broadcast time, there was provision for a unilateral contact, to occur on a specified frequency at a given time on the night prior to the bilateral contact. Acknowledgment of the receipt of the unilateral message would, thus, be made by the receiving party during the subsequent bilateral session. Unilateral contacts, offering greater security from direction finding, increased in number, and the bilateral contacts decreased, as these operations progressed.

In addition, the agent was provided with a schedule of "control calls" (about 12 a month) in which the "Centre" went on the air at certain times and the agent responded only if he had a message. If he had nothing to send, it was not necessary for him to stand by for such calls.

The call letters used by the agent for all transmissions

- 51 -

are changed with each broadcast—as are the call letters of the control station in the regular bilateral contacts—and are based on a formula derived from the calendar day and month.

The cipher systems used in the operations in question conform generally to those described earlier in this paper. The plain text is converted into numbers, the key to which is in a memorized code word. In the second stage reference is made to a key book, and a second set of numbers is obtained. The two products are added, and the final cipher obtained. A variation of this system was used also in these operations, in which the numerals in the latter stage were then transposed into letters of the alphabet, and the message as transmitted is in letters rather than numbers.

The key books used in the operations in question were popular editions of current fiction, and they were not changed frequently. In one instance the same key book was in use for over two years. The agent (and this appears to be typical practice) selected the book to be used, purchased two copies, kept one for himself, and transmitted the other to the "Centre" by courier.

Radio contact was established on an average of five or six times a month, for brief and urgent operational traffic and administrative matters such as the receipt of funds by courier, the dispatch

- 52 -

of film by courier, and arrangements for courier meetings.

During the early period of the operations in question regular courier liaison, with personal meetings, occurred about once a month, later being reduced to three-month intervals. Such meetings were stipulated as to time, place, and recognition signals; and it was in this manner that funds and equipment were brought in to the operating group and the bulkier reports and documents were transmitted to the "Centre." Both operations made use of 35 mm. film for some of their transmissions.

The chief of one of the groups, after a year in operation, was called to an adjoining country, where he was in direct contact with a superior. He was instructed to prepare a detailed report of his organizational work and full account of his operational activities for the year. This report required about 15 days to prepare, and on its completion he was instructed to return to his operation.

While in direct contact with his superior organization, however, this agent was instructed on his return to operations to prepare a series of "letter boxes" (hiding places or caches to which we have referred in the operations in Sweden), and to submit plans and photographs on each for approval. These, of course, were to

- 53 -

eliminate personal contact between couriers and network members.
Four such locations were selected and submitted, one a hole in a
pile of stones in a city park, and the others in remote places outside
of the city. Two were approved, including the one in the park, but it
appears that they never were used; instead, personal meetings with
couriers continued. However, in the companion operation one "letter
box" was used. The "Centre" notified the "illegal resident" by radio
that funds would be deposited for him in a hiding place; and, although
he had three prepared and approved caches, the "Centre" chose to
establish a new one for this deposit. He was given detailed instructions for locating a brick wall in which one brick was missing. By
reaching deeply into this hole, the agent found the package. It might
be noted that U. S. currency was supplied in this instance.

The "letter box" cache is not a new development in
Soviet intelligence technique, but until recently is not known to have
been used in the United States. (Parcel lockers have been used to
make transfers, a variation of this idea.) However, in recent Soviet
operations here the practice has been discussed or employed in
three separate instances. When used it is usually accompanied by
a signal mark in chalk or pencil indicating to the other party that a
"deposit" is waiting to be picked up. When one party wishes to meet

- 54 -

with the other, this may be indicated by placing a mark on a particular page of a public telephone book or other accessible public document.

Another twist on current operating methods is noted in the case which led to the conviction of 22 persons for espionage in Greece during the past year. Two clandestine agent radio stations located in private dwellings were uncovered in this case by direction-finding equipment. Both were concealed in basement crypts or vaults, the entrances to which were hidden. In one case a sliding concrete block covered the entrance, and in the other a door step, which could be bolted into place from within, covered the entrance. In the first house the tenants led the police immediately to the crypt; but in the other, although the station was in operation when the raid began, it was many hours before the raiding party located the crypt and then only with aid of mine-detecting equipment. A Greek Communist leader, in the crypt when it was located, shot and killed himself before the police gained entrance. Before that, however, smoke was observed coming from a chimney; and, realizing that the operator was burning his documents, the police poured water down on the fire and thus salvaged some material, including key books which subsequently were of assistance in breaking back traffic.

- 55 -

Automatic Transmitters

The most recent and the outstanding Soviet achievement in clandestine communications is the development of an automatic tape transmitter, capable of sending up to 500 words a minute, adapted for use in conjunction with the "Tensor M" type equipment. Such equipment, which will fit readily into a piece of luggage 18 inches in length, has been placed in use by Soviet intelligence.

An entirely new problem is therefore presented to the direction-finding services. The hand-keyed agent radio of the past averaged 10 to 15 words per minute, and his broadcasts were measured in terms of an hour or less. The automatic equipment will enable him to get on and off the air in a very few minutes.

A statement cannot be made as to the extent of the use of this automatic equipment in Soviet operations, nor can its technical performance be judged at the present time. It promises, however, to relieve the main weakness in Soviet clandestine communications and to offer prospect for greater use of agent radio in the future.

Microdots

Special emphasis has been given in this study of Soviet

- 56 -

communications to agent radio and its auxiliary, the clandestine courier, because the operations studied have given prominence to these mediums. This is not to discount the possibilities of the micro-dot. Akhmedov, to whom we have referred previously, has stated that the microdot process was known to the "Fourth Department" (Soviet Military Intelligence) in 1940, and related a specific instance of its use at that time. One Volnuchin was dispatched to the United States as a resident late in 1940, and was given a letter to deliver to the Military Attache at Washington. The cover text was in the form of a letter from a relative; the microdot was placed over an "i." Akhmedov recalled that Volnuchin lost the letter en route, and on reporting the fact was recalled from Washington and dismissed from the service.

It can be assumed that the Soviet intelligence services have added the German know-how in this field, and that effective use of it can now be made in their operations.

Secret Inks and Open Code

Although the technical aspects of secret ink communication are not proper to this study, it is necessary that attention be

- 57 -

directed to it as a medium. Brief reference has been made to the

enciphered messages in secret inks in the traffic between Soviet net-

works in South America and New York during the early 1940's, and

it has been noted that training in this subject was given prospective

GRU "residents" in 1945. Lacking the speed of radio and the capacity

of a courier system, secret ink communication might be looked upon

as an auxiliary or emergency medium.

Another form of written communication which must be

considered, and which cannot be fully treated herein, is open code.

This is a general term for the practice of concealing messages with-

in innocuous appearing personal correspondence or other cover texts.

This may be effected in a number of ways; cryptic words, symbols,

or letters having special markings or positions, all forms of open

code, usually are arranged privately to cover contingent situations.

Situations which have not been provided for occasion

the use of double-meaning language, another form of open code, and

for this reason it is of particular interest. It is insecure and dan-

gerous, and its use indicates an emergency. Rachel Duebendorfer's

communications with Hermina Rabinowitch in Canada, necessitated

by the fact that she was completely cut off, illustrate the use of

- 58 -

double-meaning language and the circumstances requiring it:

> We live in the former apartment and are working
> as previously in the old firm... Relations with Lucy
> are good... Sisi's (Duebendorfer) position is sad.
> Please inform Gisel's parents (Soviet Embassy at
> Ottawa) that they must remit 6,700 dollars....
> (Report of the Royal Commission, p. 571)

A few weeks later Duebendorfer sent another appeal

via Rabinowitch:

> ...Please inform Gisel's family, that she should
> advise Znamensky 19 that Sisi is alive and works
> as of old with Lucy...For the work of Sisi Gisel's
> family must transfer 10,000 dollars....
> (Ibid., p. 573)

The reference in the second letter to "Znamensky 19,"

the Moscow headquarters address of the GRU, was considered

particularly indiscreet by Soviet intelligence officials in Ottawa.

Conclusion

In summary, the main links between Soviet networks

and the "Centre" are provided by the legal communications system

of Soviet missions. Since greater security, speed, and capacity are

offered, the official channels will be used as long as they are available.

- 59 -

When cut off from official channels in the past, Soviet networks have turned to agent radio; and, where it was possible to do so, augmented the radio system by a courier link with an accessible Soviet mission in a neighboring country. Under clandestine conditions, the future prospect would seem to be for heavier reliance upon agent radio if automatic transmitting equipment proves to be effective. Courier systems will be necessary to sustain operations over a long period of time, and the microdot and secret ink processes may in some instances replace the 35 mm. film in the hands of the courier. Emergency situations may call for the use of such devices as open code on occasion. But the rigid centralization which is a trademark of Soviet operations will require the rapid exchanges in basic communications that only radio can provide.

This would seem to have an application to Soviet operations in the United States should a break in relations occur, and it must be assumed that plans for an agent radio system to function under such conditions have been formulated.

- 60 -

Milton Keynes UK
Ingram Content Group UK Ltd.
UKHW051527280324
440101UK00014B/917